To my Dear
Kathryn.

love

THE TEN COMMANDMENTS

THE SCULPTURE RELIEFS OF THE

Ten Commandments

BY CHAIM GROSS

AT INTERNATIONAL SYNAGOGUE

JOHN F. KENNEDY INTERNATIONAL AIRPORT, NEW YORK

INTRODUCTION AND TEXT BY RABBI ISRAEL MOWSHOWITZ

PUBLISHED BY INTERNATIONAL SYNAGOGUE, JAMAICA, NEW YORK

First Printing August 1973
Library of Congress Catalogue Card Number 73-83023
Printed in Italy
Designed by Abe Lerner

The International Synagogue

IS DEEPLY GRATEFUL TO

MR. AND MRS. JOSEPH MEYERHOFF

of Baltimore, Maryland *

WHOSE GENEROUS CONTRIBUTION MADE IT

POSSIBLE TO BRING TO OUR SANCTUARY

THE BEAUTY AND DIGNITY OF THESE

OUTSTANDING WORKS OF ART

The Ten Commandments

AND The Holy Ark

* To the same donors we owe the publication of this beautiful book

The International Synagogue

THE INTERNATIONAL SYNAGOGUE stands in the Tri-Faith Plaza of Kennedy Airport, directly across from the International Arrivals Building, side by side with the Protestant and Catholic Chapels, as a proud symbol of the Judeo-Christian tradition which is the foundation stone upon which American democracy had been erected.

What does America mean to the world? In most countries, America symbolizes the affluent society. It represents technological skill, gadgetry and the easy life. It stands for the most modern planes and for the most sophisticated inventions. In sum, America is for hundreds of millions in the world the embodiment of military power and economic strength.

And yet, we who love America and know it best know that our country has something far more precious to sell than the latest planes and the abundance of the products of a mass production economy. Our country was founded on an idea, on the yearning of men to establish on these shores a society of freedom dedicated to the proposition that all men are created equal and that liberty and justice are the birthright of every citizen.

Throughout our history as a nation, we held fast to this American dream. Amidst all our falterings and gropings, we never ceased to labor for the perfection of the democratic ideal.

The world doesn't know us when it thinks of us as a practical people whose symbol is the dollar sign. We are a nation of idealists who desire to perfect the world under the sovereignty of God.

The International Synagogue and its two companion chapels are, therefore, an appropriate symbol of the essence of America. The first sight that greets the 30 million visitors who pass through Kennedy Airport annually is the view of three chapels that are a witness, poured in concrete, to the commitment of our country to the dignity of man and the freedom of worship and conscience. The three chapels are a symbol to the world that America places not the material but the spiritual at the core of its being and yearning.

The Jewish community in America is a small minority in comparison with the Protestant and Catholic communities. The travelers to our shores who visit these three chapels, which are equal in size and complement one another with their beauty and dignity, see in this America's awareness that in matters of the spirit there is no minority or majority and that in our blessed land everyone has the right to express himself freely in his own way in his approach to his God and his faith.

Countless Jewish travelers have found in the International Synagogue a home away from home. The Ferkauf museum, containing art objects from every Jewish community in the world, reminds the visitor of the warm religious fellowship that unites all Jews in service to God and fellowman. The Ferkauf library is stocked with books and periodicals in many languages and from many countries, thus giving the visitor an opportunity to catch up with the latest news of his home country. The meditation room has been especially provided for quiet and prayerful contemplation. Last, but not least, the Sanctuary in which the Ten Commandments are situated is a place of solace and inspiration to the traveler.

Both Jewish and non-Jewish visitors are provided through the International Synagogue with a glimpse into the nobility and meaningfulness of the Jewish way of life.

Introduction

WHEN WOODROW WILSON proposed his 14 points at the Versailles Conference, Clemenceau observed that Mr. Wilson was more demanding than Moses; for Moses gave the world only Ten Commandments while he, Wilson, was advocating 14 points. Mr. Wilson replied: "Mr. Clemenceau, if you will promise that the world will accept the Ten Commandments, I will gladly give up my 14 points."

The Ten Commandments have become the moral and ethical guide for mankind. They wielded an unparalleled influence upon the development of civilization. The 120 words in the Hebrew version of the Decalogue served humanity as the building bricks for a more hopeful future.

When the children of Israel gathered about Mount Sinai in preparation for the revelation, "there were thunders and lightnings, and a thick cloud upon the Mount, and the voice of a horn exceeding loud; and all the people that were in the camp trembled." Our Sages inform us that the nations of the world were frightened by these extraordinary occurrences. They feared lest God bring another deluge upon the earth, either a deluge of fire or a deluge of water. A voice was then heard proclaiming: "God is bringing strength to His people; God will bless His people with peace." It is through the observance of the Ten Commandments that the world is to achieve the prayed-for peace. The ways of the revelation are "ways of pleasantness, and all its paths are peace."

Jewish tradition has embellished the event of the revelation with many beautiful spiritual insights. The Tablets upon which the Ten Commandments were inscribed were prepared before creation so that mankind may know that the moral law contained in the Ten Commandments is independent of time and independent of man. The Ten Commandments were given at Sinai in the desert, a place that belongs to no one and therefore belongs to all; to teach us that the moral law is not the property of one people, but that it belongs to all mankind.

The voice which proclaimed the Ten Commandments miraculously divided into 70 voices speaking all the 70 languages of men. All mankind was to hear and to understand the message of the Decalogue. Furthermore, for those who could not comprehend the message, there was a beautiful symbolic lesson. The Torah containing the Ten Commandments and a sword came down together from heaven and a voice was heard to proclaim, "You must make your choice: either you choose the sword or you choose the book. You cannot have both."

The revelation took place in the month of Sivan because the sign of the zodiac of this month is a twin and man, too, is a twin. There are twin forces operating within man, the good inclination and the evil inclination. The moral law was given to man so that, guided by it, he may be able to triumph over his evil inclination and to express himself through his good inclination. The Rabbis describe to us a picturesque scene in heaven when the angels protested to the Almighty against giving the Ten Commandments to man. They considered the moral law to be too sacred to be given to mere mortals. God, however, replied that angels are not subject to temptations; angels do not steal nor do they rob or commit adultery. It is man who needs the moral law in order to be able to resist temptation and to overcome his evil inclination and through the moral law to reach out to the good and to the blessed life.

The Rabbis observe that the first five commandments contain duties pertaining to the relation of man to his God while the last five commandments written on the second tablet of the law contain duties pertaining to the relation of man to his fellowman. Both are necessary for human happiness. Furthermore, the Rabbis point out, the Hebrew word for "tablets" is written in the singular in order to emphasize the truth that for the complete life one must fulfill one's duties both to God and to fellowman and that the neglect of one of these makes for a splintered, fragmented life.

The Rabbis found a close and intimate correspondence between the first five commandments written on one tablet and the last five commandments written on the other tablet. The first commandment, "I am the Lord Thy God," corresponds to the sixth commandment, "Thou shalt not murder." It is God who gives life, it is God who is the creator of life and it is He who had fashioned man in His own image; therefore man has no right to take the life of another man.

The second commandment, "Thou shalt have no other Gods before me," corresponds to the seventh commandment, "Thou shalt not commit adultery." Thus does the prophet, Hosea, to demonstrate the Jewish people's unfaithfulness to God, marry a well known prostitute, Gomer, thereby indicating that unfaithfulness to God may be equated with unfaithfulness in the relation between man and woman.

The third commandment, "Thou shalt not take the name of the Lord Thy God in vain," corresponds to the eighth commandment, "Thou shalt not steal." When one uses the name of God meanly and cheaply, one steals from God's glory; one diminishes God's grandeur.

The fourth commandment, "Remember the Sabbath day to keep it holy," corresponds to the ninth commandment, "Thou shalt not bear false witness against they neighbor." The Sabbath is, of course, a reminder and a witness of the existence of God who created the earth in six days and rested on the Sabbath, the seventh day. Those who do not keep the Sabbath bear false witness against God by denying the testimony of the Sabbath to the works of creation, thus bearing false witness against God as man so often bears false witness against his neighbor.

The fifth commandment, "Honor thy father and thy mother," corresponds to the tenth commandment, "Thou shalt not covet they neighbor's house; thou shalt not covet thy neighbor's wife." For both these commandments speak about the importance of pure, loyal and noble family relationships.

The Rabbis dwelt at length and lovingly upon every sentence, every word and every letter of the Ten Commandments. They explored the meaning of every commandment and discovered in the Decalogue a most effective guide for life. Thus, for example, did they interpret the commandment, "Thou shalt not steal," not only to mean stealing of material things, but also stealing of another man's reputation or, through false pretenses, stealing another man's good will. They found in the Ten Commandments hidden meanings, allusions, and allusions of allusions. The more they studied, the more they discovered the inner hidden light of the Commandments.

The central theme of the Sanctuary of the International Synagogue is the Ten Commandments. It consists of ten individual panels, each measuring 42 by 30 inches. They form one unit which succeeds admirably in conveying the sense of the sublime power and inspiration of the Decalogue. The panels are sculptured in bronze with gold overleaf and are the works of one of the greatest artists of our time, Chaim Gross.

Mr. Gross was confronted by a very difficult challenge. He had to capture eternity in time and the infinite in the finite space. He had to convey the simple meaning of the Decalogue and to make a clear statement of them but he also needed to leave the sculpture open to interpretations and limitless explorations. He captured in the sculpture the very spirit of Jewish tradition and its reverence for God's word. He created a work of art of which the viewer never tires and which he never sees in the same way twice. There are always new intimations, new mysteries, new allusions. One is struck by the power of the truth of the

Ten Commandments as one views the sculpture, but one also feels echoes and echoes of echoes of truths yet to be discovered and yet to be revealed. Like any truly great work of art, the more one views the Ten Commandments, the more one appreciates them, the more one is challenged by them.

Let us now proceed to a brief description of the individual panels.

THE HOLY ARK is a beautiful and inspiring complement to the Ten Commandments.

Above the Ark, underneath the Eternal Lamp, there are written the words "Holy, Holy, Holy." The words are intertwined and executed in such a fashion as to give the impression of something growing and proliferating. It is not difficult to conceive of the letters as roots of trees. As we look upon the inscription, there is brought to our minds forcibly the Biblical statement that the Torah is "A tree of life to them that grasp it."

In the center of the Ark doors, the artist placed the Hebrew letter "Hei." This letter is in Jewish tradition often substituted for the full spelling of the name of God. Out of this letter there radiate rays in all directions symbolizing the power of faith and the strength that the believer derives from the Torah. The rays also symbolize the light of truth, for the Torah is truth, and the stamp of the Almighty is truth.

God reveals Himself not only in nature, but also and especially in the affairs of nations and men. That is why the first commandment does not speak about God as the creator, but as the great redeemer from bondage. This thought was beautifully captured by the artist through the portrayal of a pyramid, a symbol of enslavement, surrounded by the healing rays of God who is merciful, compassionate and the great redeemer. One can see within the rays of light the formation of an eye symbolic of the watchful eye of the Almighty who saw the suffering of the children of Israel in Egyptian bondage and heeded their cry for help. Underneath there are symbolic flames reminding us of the comparison, by the Rabbis, of the Torah to fire; for just as fire purifies, so does the word of God purify and ennoble.

FIRST COMMANDMENT. "I am the Lord Thy God who brought thee out of the land of Egypt, out of the house of bondage."

There are, of course, many forms of idolatry, but the worship of the golden calf is the most common. That which we place as the priority of our hopes and aspirations can be truly said to be our God; and to many mammon is God. One observes in the panel the hammers breaking up the idol and the snake at the bottom which represents the enticer. Here you have an allusion to the common denominator between idolatry and adultery. It is the snake that first broke up an idyllic family life in the Garden of Eden when he beguiled Eve to convince Adam to eat from the forbidden tree. The bird, which is in this instance a dove, is symbolic of faithfulness or chastity. Jewish tradition speaks of the dove as a monogamous bird and thus does the dove, in juxtaposition to the snake and the golden idol, symbolize constancy and faithfulness to God.

SECOND COMMANDMENT. "Thou shalt have no other Gods before me."

The artist succeeds most amazingly in making very real and concrete to us this abstract idea.

The name by which we know God is our concept of God. When our God idea is small, when the eternal and all-encompassing is placed in narrow limits of space and time, then indeed do we take the name of the Lord our God in vain. We have a false, inadequate and untrue image of the Almighty.

This thought is conveyed by the artist when he places the open Torah at the center of this panel. The name of the Lord is truth, the Rabbis tell us. The very signature of the Lord is truth, they assert. The Torah symbolizes truth and to take the name of the Lord in vain means to be untrue to God, to have a false concept of Him. The Torah is God's revealed truth which contains a true reflection of his everlasting glory and the finger is the finger of God as He reveals His greatness and His truth in the affairs of nations and men. Here a powerful-looking bird spreads its wings heavenward as if to lift our gaze onward and upward and to raise our vision of God. Again underneath the panel there are the flames symbolizing the purifying power of the fire of the true faith.

THIRD COMMANDMENT. "Thou shalt not take the name of the Lord thy God in vain."

In the right-hand corner of the panel, one can see the two Sabbath candles burning. The center of the panel is taken up by imaginative forms of angels with their backs towards each other. This is based on the beautiful Rabbinic legend that the angel of good and angel of evil visit each Jewish home on the Sabbath eve. If they see peace in the home and love and devotion of the members of the family one to the other, then the good angel pronounces a blessing and the angel of evil perforce answers, "Amen." On the other hand, should the angels find that there is discord in the family and there is the absence of the spirit of Sabbath peace, then the angel of evil pronounces a malediction and the angel of good perforce answers, "Amen." Significantly, all the lines seem to be flowing upwards, vertically, to make our gaze travel higher and thus to remind us that the purpose of the Sabbath is to lift man's heart and to sensitize him to the higher values of life.

FOURTH COMMANDMENT. "Remember the Sabbath Day, to keep it holy."

There are discernible in the panel two abstract human forms representing father and mother and to the right of the panel there is an abstract form that looks like a child. The child brings flowers to the father and mother as a token of its love and respect for the parents. There is above them the bird spreading its wings in protection of the family unit. The bird in this instance seems to be a dove which in Jewish tradition and especially in the Song of Songs represents love. The entire panel reflects a sense of strength, love and peace.

FIFTH COMMANDMENT. "Honor thy father and thy mother, that thy days may be long upon the land which the Lord thy God giveth thee."

This panel needs no interpretation. It is a most powerful statement of the crime of murder. The ultimate evil of murder is represented by the mushroom of the atom bomb which murders indiscriminately without passion and without even knowing its victims. The longer one views this panel, the more one gets the feeling of utter destruction, of ultimate tragedy. There is transmitted in it a sense of nothingness, of disintegration, of a falling apart.

SIXTH COMMANDMENT. "Thou shalt not murder."

One sees the outline of a home and in it two birds. These two birds face each other, are attracted one to the other, but are at the same time also repelled by one another. They want to come close but there is also a force that keeps them apart. Around them are the forms of angelic wings as if to underscore the duality of the relationship. Adultery is man living at his lowest level, expressing unfaithfulness as represented by the attraction of the two birds. On the other hand, the wings are symbolic of the capacity of man to rise above his temptations. Indeed, by resisting temptation, man is like unto the angels.

SEVENTH COMMANDMENT. "Thou shalt not commit adultery."

One can see a hand grabbing hold of another hand, the hand of the thief, and one can discern coins falling from the thief's hand. The interesting thing about this panel is that the artist is stating for us a great truth. What he is saying is not only that man should not steal, but that, indeed, man cannot steal. The coins are falling from the hand to show that the thief has gained nothing. Gains through dishonesty are not kept for long. What man obtains dishonestly he will not and cannot keep for long.

EIGHTH COMMANDMENT. "Thou shalt not steal."

The open Torah is a witness to the truth. The Torah is a witness to God's revelation and to God's truth.

The Torah together with the Hebrew letter, "Tet", form an oil lamp to remind us that the Torah is a light which dispels the darkness of ignorance and gives us the ability to see the truth. The hand which seems to say "Stop" is a powerful hand which not only conveys the idea that man must stop bearing false witness, but also that man becomes strong by telling the truth.

NINTH COMMANDMENT. "Thou shalt not bear false witness against thy neighbor."

The Rabbis tell us that the heart and the eye are the two brokers of sin: the eye sees and the heart covets. Here you note the hand covering the eye so that the eye might not see and the heart might not covet. There is also evident in the lower right-hand corner of the panel the head of an angel in bird form with wings spreading surrounding the eye. Again, this is a reminder to man that he was born for greatness and that by resisting evil and by overcoming the temptation to covet that which is not his, he fulfills his highest destiny. The eye in the angel is clear and uncovered in contrast to the covered eye of man. Again, this is a powerful contrast between an eye that sees evil, an eye that covets, and an eye that clearly looks at the noblest and most appealing aspects of the good and godly life.

TENTH COMMANDMENT. "Thou shalt not covet."

Chaim Gross, American Artist

CHAIM GROSS looks exactly as we imagine an artist ought to look. His cherubic face, kind yet suffused with strength, his warm, sympathetic eyes, ruddy complexion and curly hair, reflect the special sensitivity of the artist. Certainly in his case it is true to say that not only does the artist fashion art, but at the same time art fashions the artist.

Chaim was born in a village in Czechoslovakia nestled in one of the beautiful green valleys of the Carpathian Mountains surrounded by forests. Here he became intoxicated with the beautiful artwork of the Supreme Artist of whom the psalmist sang, "The heavens declare the glory of God, and the firmament showeth His handiwork." It is in the forests of his native village that Chaim learned to appreciate the special qualities inherent in the various types of wood in which he was to do much of his sculpture.

His father's home was a warm, traditional Jewish home with a strongly Chassidic background. It was a happy home, filled with the joy and strength of faith and the poetry of ceremonial practices and observances.

During the First World War, he witnessed a pogrom perpetrated by drunken Cossacks. He became a refugee and wandered far and wide, sleeping often in open fields and ditches.

His love of art accompanied him along the way. As a lad of fifteen, while living as a refugee in Budapest, he already won a competition for admission to an art school, being chosen as one out of four hundred and fifty candidates. When he arrived in the United States, he accepted all kinds of odd jobs, never taking full employment so that he might devote himself to his art. He has won many national honors and gained national and international recognition for his work as sculptor and painter.

The two most dominant influences in Chaim's life were the Holocaust and the State of Israel. The Holocaust awakened in him repressed memories of the pogroms that he witnessed in his native village and which found expression in the fantasy that one sees so often in his work. The State of Israel brought back echoes of the joy and happiness in the Jewish traditional practices Chaim knew in his childhood home. His art is the distillation and objectivization of his experiences. It is an expression of personal, traumatic, and meaningful moments transformed by the artist into universal language.

In recent years Chaim has been devoting himself to Jewish themes. His work reminds one of John Ruskin's observation. "When love and skill work together, expect a masterpiece." Chaim's deep love for Jewish values, harnessed to his artistic skill, has produced many masterpieces on Jewish themes including, of course, the sculpture reliefs for the Ten Commandments. The amazing aspect of his work on Jewish themes, however, is that while they are rooted deeply in Jewish tradition, Chaim succeeds in having them convey a universal message.

Kahlil Gibran once observed that "Art is one step from the visibly known toward the unknown." Chaim's special ability is to reveal to us unknown worlds of feeling, meaning, and beauty.